HOW MUCH DO YOU
EACH OTHER? LET'... ....ᵔ ᵔ ᵔ ᵔ:

Communication is key in a relationship, and what better way to ignite fun conversations and connect with each other than by asking the important questions...and the not-so-deep ones too!

We hope you enjoy the ride, and we hope this book brings you even closer.

1. What's the first thing you noticed about each other?

_____
_____
_____
_____
_____
_____
_____
_____
_____
_____

2. Who is more of a risk taker?

_____
_____
_____
_____
_____
_____
_____
_____
_____
_____

LOVE DOES NOT DOMINATE; IT CULTIVATES
-JOHANN WOLFGANG VON GOETHE

3. WHAT ARE YOU MOST SENTIMENTAL ABOUT?

_____
_____
_____
_____
_____
_____
_____
_____
_____
_____

4. WHAT THREE WORDS BEST DESCRIBE YOU?

_____
_____
_____
_____
_____
_____
_____
_____
_____
_____

LOVE IS THE WHOLE THING. WE ARE ONLY PIECES
– RUMI

5. WHAT DO YOU LOOK FORWARD TO MOST IN THE DAY?

_____
_____
_____
_____
_____
_____
_____
_____
_____

6. WHAT IS YOUR BIGGEST REGRET?

_____
_____
_____
_____
_____
_____
_____
_____
_____

 TO LOVE AN BE LOVED, IS TO FEEL THE SUN FROM BOTH SIDES
- DAVID VISCOTT

7. WHAT DO YOU THINK ARE YOUR BEST AND WORST PERSONALITY TRAITS?

_____
_____
_____
_____
_____
_____
_____
_____
_____
_____

8. WHAT ANIMAL ARE YOU MOST AFRAID OF?

_____
_____
_____
_____
_____
_____
_____
_____
_____
_____

LIFE IS THE FLOWER, FOR WHICH LOVE IS THE HONEY
- VICTOR HUGO

9. WHAT DO YOU WANT TO BE REMEMBERED FOR?

_____
_____
_____
_____
_____
_____
_____
_____
_____

10. IF YOU HAD ALL THE MONEY TO OPEN A BUSINESS, WHAT TYPE WOULD IT BE?

_____
_____
_____
_____
_____
_____
_____
_____
_____

ALL THAT YOU ARE IS ALL THAT I'LL EVER NEED
- ED SHEERAN

11. WHAT IS YOUR WEAKNESS?

_____
_____
_____
_____
_____
_____
_____
_____
_____

12. WHAT SCHOOL SUBJECT DID YOU LIKE AND HATE THE MOST?

_____
_____
_____
_____
_____
_____
_____
_____
_____

LOVE RECOGNIZES NO BARRIERS
- MAYA ANGELOU

13. WHAT IS YOUR EARLIEST MEMORY?

_____
_____
_____
_____
_____
_____
_____
_____
_____
_____

14. WHAT DO I DO THAT MAKES YOU THE HAPPIEST?

_____
_____
_____
_____
_____
_____
_____
_____
_____
_____

WE ARE MOST ALIVE WHEN WE'RE IN LOVE
- JOHN UPDIKE

15. WHAT IS YOUR FAVORITE WAY WE SPEND TIME TOGETHER?

_____
_____
_____
_____
_____
_____
_____
_____
_____
_____

16. WHEN WAS THE LAST TIME THAT YOU CRIED?

_____
_____
_____
_____
_____
_____
_____
_____
_____
_____

LOVE IS FRIENDSHIP THAT HAS CAUGHT FIRE
- ANN LANDERS

17. IF YOU COULD INSTANTLY LEARN A TALENT/SKILL, WHAT WOULD IT BE?

_____
_____
_____
_____
_____
_____
_____
_____
_____
_____

18. WHAT WAS YOUR FAVORITE TOY AS A CHILD?

_____
_____
_____
_____
_____
_____
_____
_____
_____
_____

19. IF YOU COULD GO BACK IN TIME, WHAT AGE WOULD YOU BE AGAIN?

_____
_____
_____
_____
_____
_____
_____
_____
_____
_____

20. WHERE WOULD BE YOUR IDEAL VACATION?

_____
_____
_____
_____
_____
_____
_____
_____
_____
_____

TRUE LOVE STORIES NEVER HAVE ENDINGS
- RICHARD BACH

21. IF YOU COULD MEET ANYONE IN THE WORLD WHO WOULD IT BE?

_____
_____
_____
_____
_____
_____
_____
_____
_____
_____

22. WHAT IS YOUR GREATEST FEAR?

_____
_____
_____
_____
_____
_____
_____
_____
_____
_____

 ABSENCE SHARPENS LOVE, PRESENCE STRENGTHENS IT
— THOMAS FULLER

23. WHAT IS THE MOST DARING THING YOU HAVE EVER DONE? WOULD YOU DO IT AGAIN?

_____
_____
_____
_____
_____
_____
_____
_____
_____

24. WHO IS MORE INCLINED TO BE JEALOUS?

_____
_____
_____
_____
_____
_____
_____
_____
_____

LOVE IS THE FLOWER; YOU'VE GOT TO LET IT GROW
- JOHN LENNON

25. WHAT SUPERPOWER DO YOU WISH YOU COULD HAVE?

_____
_____
_____
_____
_____
_____
_____
_____
_____
_____

26. WHAT IS YOUR BIGGEST PET PEEVE? ABOUT ME AND IN GENERAL.

_____
_____
_____
_____
_____
_____
_____
_____
_____
_____

27. IF YOU COULD CHANGE ONE THING ABOUT YOURSELF, WHAT WOULD IT BE?

_____
_____
_____
_____
_____
_____
_____
_____
_____
_____

28. WHAT IS YOUR HAPPIEST MEMORY ABOUT OUR RELATIONSHIP?

_____
_____
_____
_____
_____
_____
_____
_____
_____
_____

IF I KNOW WHAT LOVE IS, IT IS BECAUSE OF YOU
- HERMANN HESSE

29. WHERE DO YOU THINK WE'LL BE IN 5 YEARS?

_____
_____
_____
_____
_____
_____
_____
_____
_____
_____

30. WHAT IS YOUR MOST ATTRACTIVE PHYSICAL TRAIT?

_____
_____
_____
_____
_____
_____
_____
_____
_____
_____

IF I KNOW WHAT LOVE IS, IT IS BECAUSE OF YOU
– HERMANN HESSE

31. WHAT IS YOUR FAVORITE SEX POSITION?

_____
_____
_____
_____
_____
_____
_____
_____
_____
_____

32. WHAT NON-SEXUAL TRAIT ABOUT ME TURNS YOU ON?

_____
_____
_____
_____
_____
_____
_____
_____
_____

33. WHAT WOULD YOU DO FOR A LIVING IF YOU COULD DO ANYTHING?

_____
_____
_____
_____
_____
_____
_____
_____
_____
_____

34. WHAT IS THE WORST MOVIE YOU HAVE EVER SEEN?

_____
_____
_____
_____
_____
_____
_____
_____
_____
_____

LOVE IS WHAT MAKES THE RIDE WORTHWHILE
- FRANKLIN P. JONES

35. WHO WOULD PLAY YOU IN A MOVIE ABOUT YOUR LIFE?

_____
_____
_____
_____
_____
_____
_____
_____
_____

36. WHAT SONG MAKES YOU THINK ABOUT ME?

_____
_____
_____
_____
_____
_____
_____
_____
_____

37. WHAT WAS YOUR DREAM JOB WHEN YOU WERE A KID?

_____
_____
_____
_____
_____
_____
_____
_____
_____
_____

38. WHAT IS YOUR LEAST FAVORITE CHORE?

_____
_____
_____
_____
_____
_____
_____
_____
_____
_____

A LIFE LIVED IN LOVE WILL NEVER BE DULL
- LEO BUSCAGLIA

39. IF YOU COULD CHOOSE YOUR NAME, WHAT WOULD IT BE?

_____
_____
_____
_____
_____
_____
_____
_____
_____
_____

40. WHAT'S YOUR FAVORITE THING ABOUT US THAT WE HAVE IN COMMON?

_____
_____
_____
_____
_____
_____
_____
_____
_____
_____

YOU CALL IT MADNESS, BUT I CALL IT LOVE
- DON BYAS

41. WHAT WOULD YOU DO IF YOU HAD ONE DAY LEFT TO LIVE?

_____
_____
_____
_____
_____
_____
_____
_____
_____
_____

42. WHAT'S YOUR FAVORITE TIME OF DAY TO HAVE SEX?

_____
_____
_____
_____
_____
_____
_____
_____
_____
_____

LOVE IS NOT LOVE UNTIL LOVE'S VULNERABLE
- THEODORE ROETHKE

43. DESCRIBE OUR RELATIONSHIP IN ONE WORD.

_____
_____
_____
_____
_____
_____
_____
_____
_____
_____

44. WHERE WERE WE WHEN WE HAD OUR FIRST KISS?

_____
_____
_____
_____
_____
_____
_____
_____
_____
_____

LOVE IS THE ULTIMATE EXPRESSION OF THE WILL TO LIVE
- TOM WOLFE

45. WHAT MADE YOU FALL IN LOVE WITH ME?

_____
_____
_____
_____
_____
_____
_____
_____
_____
_____

46. WHAT BOTHERS YOU THE MOST ABOUT ME?

_____
_____
_____
_____
_____
_____
_____
_____
_____
_____

YOU CALL IT MADNESS, BUT I CALL IT LOVE
– DON BYAS

47. IF YOU HAD A TIME MACHINE, WOULD YOU GO BACK OR INTO THE FUTURE?

_____
_____
_____
_____
_____
_____
_____
_____
_____
_____

48. IF YOU HAD $1 MILLION DOLLARS TODAY, HOW WOULD YOU SPEND IT?

_____
_____
_____
_____
_____
_____
_____
_____
_____
_____

WHEN ONE LOVES, ONE DOES NOT CALCULATE
- SAINT THERESE OF LISIEUX

49. WHAT WOULD YOUR DREAM HOUSE LOOK LIKE?

_____
_____
_____
_____
_____
_____
_____
_____
_____

50. WHAT IS YOUR CRAZIEST FANTASY?

_____
_____
_____
_____
_____
_____
_____
_____
_____
_____

GROW OLD WITH ME! THE BEST IS YET TO BE
- ROBERT BROWNING

51. WHAT IS THE ONE THING YOU WOULD NEVER FORGIVE IN A RELATIONSHIP?

_____
_____
_____
_____
_____
_____
_____
_____
_____
_____

52. WHAT DOES THE WORD 'LOVE' MEAN TO YOU?

_____
_____
_____
_____
_____
_____
_____
_____
_____
_____

 WHAT THE WORLD NEEDS IS MORE LOVE AND LESS PAPERWORK
- PEARL BAILEY

53. WHERE WOULD YOU LIKE TO RETIRE?

_____

_____

_____

_____

_____

_____

_____

_____

_____

54. WHAT IS ONE THING ON YOUR BUCKET LIST YOU MUST DO BEFORE YOU'RE GONE?

_____

_____

_____

_____

_____

_____

_____

_____

_____

 'TIS BETTER TO HAVE LOVED AND LOST, THAN NEVER TO HAVE LOVED AT ALL
- ALFRED, LORD TENNYSON

55. DO YOU BELIEVE IN GOD?

_____
_____
_____
_____
_____
_____
_____
_____
_____
_____

56. IF YOU COULD SWAP LIVES WITH ONE PERSON FOR A DAY, WHO WOULD IT BE?

_____
_____
_____
_____
_____
_____
_____
_____
_____
_____

 TO LOVE SOMEONE IS TO SEE A MIRACLE INVISIBLE TO OTHERS
— FRANCOIS MAURIAC

57. WHAT WOULD YOU CHANGE ABOUT OUR RELATIONSHIP, IF ANYTHING?

_____
_____
_____
_____
_____
_____
_____
_____
_____

58. WHAT HAS BEEN THE MOST EMBARRASSING MOMENT IN YOUR LIFE?

_____
_____
_____
_____
_____
_____
_____
_____
_____

59. WHAT IS THE BEST ADVICE YOU'VE EVER BEEN GIVEN?

_____

_____

_____

_____

_____

_____

_____

_____

_____

60. WHAT HABIT WOULD YOU LIKE TO CHANGE ABOUT YOURSELF?

_____

_____

_____

_____

_____

_____

_____

_____

_____

 WHATEVER OUR SOULS ARE MADE OF, HIS AND MINE ARE THE SAME
- EMILY BRONTE

61. WOULD YOU LIKE TO HAVE KIDS ONE DAY? OR MORE KIDS?

_____
_____
_____
_____
_____
_____
_____
_____
_____

62. WHAT ACCOMPLISHMENT ARE YOU THE MOST PROUD OF?

_____
_____
_____
_____
_____
_____
_____
_____
_____

IN LOVE THERE ARE TWO THINGS—BODIES AND WORDS
- JOYCE CAROL OATES

63. IF YOU WERE GRANTED 3 WISHES RIGHT NOW, WHAT WOULD THEY BE?

_____
_____
_____
_____
_____
_____
_____
_____
_____
_____

64. WHAT IS ONE THING YOU'RE SCARED TO ASK ME, BUT WANT TO KNOW?

_____
_____
_____
_____
_____
_____
_____
_____
_____
_____

LOVE MAKES YOUR SOUL CRAWL OUT FROM ITS HIDING PLACE
- ZORA NEALE HURSTON

65. DO YOU BELIEVE EVERYTHING HAPPENS FOR A REASON?

_____
_____
_____
_____
_____
_____
_____
_____
_____

66. WHAT WOULD BE YOUR IDEAL ROMANTIC DATE?

_____
_____
_____
_____
_____
_____
_____
_____
_____

 HAVE ENOUGH COURAGE TO TRUST LOVE ONE MORE TIME AND ALWAYS ONE MORE TIME
- MAYA ANGELOU

67. IF YOU COULD SEE INTO THE FUTURE, WHAT IS ONE THING YOU WOULD LIKE TO KNOW?

_____

_____

_____

_____

_____

_____

_____

_____

_____

_____

68. WHAT IS YOUR FAVORITE WAY TO RECEIVE AFFECTION?

_____

_____

_____

_____

_____

_____

_____

_____

_____

_____

NEVER LOVE ANYONE WHO TREATS YOU LIKE YOU'RE ORDINARY
- OSCAR WILDE

69. WHAT WAS THE FIRST THING WE SAID TO EACH OTHER?

_____
_____
_____
_____
_____
_____
_____
_____
_____
_____

70. WHAT IS ONE THING I DO THAT YOU WILL NEVER GET TIRED OF?

_____
_____
_____
_____
_____
_____
_____
_____
_____
_____

 LOVE IS AN IRRESISTIBLE DESIRE TO BE IRRESISTIBLY DESIRED
- ROBERT FROST

71. DO YOU DREAM ABOUT ME, AND IF SO WHAT WAS THE LAST THING YOU DREAMT?

_____
_____
_____
_____
_____
_____
_____
_____
_____
_____

72. WHAT IS YOUR FAVORITE THING YOU LIKE TO SEE ME WEARING?

_____
_____
_____
_____
_____
_____
_____
_____
_____
_____

 LOVE IS COMPOSED OF A SINGLE SOUL INHABITING TWO BODIES
- ARISTOTLE

73. WHAT IS YOUR FAVORITE SCENT?

_____
_____
_____
_____
_____
_____
_____
_____
_____
_____

74. WHAT WOULD BE THE PERFECT MEAL FOR YOU?

_____
_____
_____
_____
_____
_____
_____
_____
_____
_____

THERE IS NO CHARM EQUAL TO TENDERNESS OF THE HEART
- JANE AUSTEN

73. WHAT IS ONE THING ABOUT ME I SEE AS A FLAW BUT YOU LOVE?

_____
_____
_____
_____
_____
_____
_____
_____
_____
_____

74. WHO IS THE MORE AFFECTIONATE IN THE RELATIONSHIP?

_____
_____
_____
_____
_____
_____
_____
_____
_____
_____

 THERE IS ONLY ONE HAPPINESS IN THIS LIFE, TO LOVE AND BE LOVED
— GEORGE SAND

75. WHAT IS ONE THING YOU CANNOT LIVE WITHOUT?

_____
_____
_____
_____
_____
_____
_____
_____
_____
_____

76. IF YOU COULD INSTANTLY LEARN A NEW LANGUAGE, WHAT WOULD IT BE?

_____
_____
_____
_____
_____
_____
_____
_____
_____
_____

77. WHAT IS THE BIGGEST MISCONCEPTION PEOPLE HAVE ABOUT YOU?

_____
_____
_____
_____
_____
_____
_____
_____
_____
_____

78. DESCRIBE THE PERFECT ROMANTIC DATE.

_____
_____
_____
_____
_____
_____
_____
_____
_____
_____

LOVE HAS NO AGE, NO LIMIT AND NO DEATH
– JOHN GALSWORTHY

79. WHAT IS ONE THING YOU WILL NEVER EAT?

_____
_____
_____
_____
_____
_____
_____
_____
_____
_____

80. TELL ME SOMETHING I DON'T KNOW ABOUT YOU.

_____
_____
_____
_____
_____
_____
_____
_____
_____
_____

LOVE IS NOT ONLY SOMETHING YOU FEEL, IT IS SOMETHING YOU DO
- DAVID WILKERSON

81. WHAT IS THE CORRECT WAY FOR TOILET PAPER TO BE PLACED ON THE ROLL?

_____
_____
_____
_____
_____
_____
_____
_____
_____
_____

82. ARE YOU A MORNING PERSON OR A NIGHT OWL?

_____
_____
_____
_____
_____
_____
_____
_____
_____
_____

 LIFE WITHOUT LOVE IS LIKE A TREE WITHOUT BLOSSOMS OR FRUIT
- KHALIL GIBRAN

83. WHAT MAKES YOU FEEL BETTER WHEN YOU ARE SAD OR MAD?

_____
_____
_____
_____
_____
_____
_____
_____
_____

84. DO YOU BELIEVE WE ARE MEANT TO BE?

_____
_____
_____
_____
_____
_____
_____
_____
_____

THE FIRST DUTY OF LOVE IS TO LISTEN
- PAUL TILLICH

85. WHAT DO YOU ADMIRE MOST ABOUT ME?

_____
_____
_____
_____
_____
_____
_____
_____
_____

86. WHAT DO YOU THINK HAPPENS AFTER WE DIE?

_____
_____
_____
_____
_____
_____
_____
_____
_____

87. WHAT IS THE MOST IMPORTANT THING I SHOULD KNOW ABOUT YOU?

_____

_____

_____

_____

_____

_____

_____

_____

_____

88. DO YOU BELIEVE THERE IS LIFE ON OTHER PLANETS?

_____

_____

_____

_____

_____

_____

_____

_____

_____

COME LIVE IN MY HEART AND PAY NO RENT
- SAMUEL LOVER

89. WOULD YOU RATHER EAT ONLY PIZZA FOR A YEAR OR NOT EAT PIZZA FOR A YEAR?

_____
_____
_____
_____
_____
_____
_____
_____
_____

90. WHICH ONE OF US WOULD SURVIVE A ZOMBIE APOCALYPSE?

_____
_____
_____
_____
_____
_____
_____
_____
_____

WHERE THERE IS LOVE THERE IS LIFE
- MAHATMA GANDHI

91. WHAT WOULD YOU BRING FOR AN ADULT SHOW AND TELL?

_____
_____
_____
_____
_____
_____
_____
_____
_____

92. WHAT MOVIE WILL YOU NEVER GET TIRED OF SEEING OVER AND OVER AGAIN?

_____
_____
_____
_____
_____
_____
_____
_____
_____

93. WHAT IS THE BEST GIFT I COULD EVER GIVE YOU?

_____
_____
_____
_____
_____
_____
_____
_____
_____
_____

94. WHAT DO YOU THINK KEEPS US TOGETHER?

_____
_____
_____
_____
_____
_____
_____
_____
_____
_____

ALL THE TOUCH OF LOVE EVERYONE BECOMES A POET
- PLATO

95. WHAT DO YOU WISH YOU HAD MORE TIME TO DO?

_____
_____
_____
_____
_____
_____
_____
_____
_____

96. WHO INSPIRES YOU THE MOST, OR WHO HAVE YOU ALWAYS LOOKED UP TO?

_____
_____
_____
_____
_____
_____
_____
_____
_____

 LOVE IS LIKE WAR; EASY TO BEGIN BUT VERY HARD TO STOP
- H. L. MENCKEN

97. WHAT IS SOMETHING YOU'LL ONLY DO IN FRONT OF ME BUT NOT OTHER PEOPLE?

_____
_____
_____
_____
_____
_____
_____
_____
_____
_____

98. WHAT JOB WOULD YOU NEVER DO?

_____
_____
_____
_____
_____
_____
_____
_____
_____
_____
_____

THE COURSE OF TRUE LOVE NEVER DID RUN SMOOTH
- WILLIAM SHAKESPEARE

99. WHAT ARE YOU MOST GRATEFUL FOR?

_____

_____

_____

_____

_____

_____

_____

_____

_____

100. WHAT IS SOMETHING YOU WANT TO DO TOGETHER WE'VE NEVER DONE BEFORE?

_____

_____

_____

_____

_____

_____

_____

_____

_____

THE BEST THING TO HOLD ONTO IN LIFE IS EACH OTHER
- AUDREY HEPBURN

COMPLETED ON

Made in United States
Orlando, FL
04 December 2024

54533763R00031